Hairstylist's Planner & Journal

The Ultimate Organizer for Professionals in Salons and Spas

This Hairstylist's Planner & Journal belongs to:

"Life is more beautiful when you meet the right hairdresser."
- Peter Coppola

writer / illustrator: Shoshana Brand

A Collection of Open Minds

Hairstylist's Planner & Journal
The Ultimate Organizer for Professionals in Salons and Spas

ISBN: 978-1-7378236-0-5
Cover design by Shoshana Brand
Made in the USA, 2021

Own a Journal to Tell Your Tale

www.ajarbooks.com

Dear journal owner;

If you are a hairstylist, you definitely have the mind of an entrepreneur, the heart of an artist, and the eye for a modern design.

You also know how to listen, and it's easy for you to communicate with all sorts of people. In other words - you are one of a kind, and you deserve the best products.

This great illustrated planner & journal will help you delve into the best within your Hairstylist Self.

Use this book from cover to cover for your everyday needs in your business and beyond. Start with any year and any day of the year, and feel free to make this journal your own.

May you always have a good hair day.

Love -

Ajar Books

Notes to Self

Where am I today?

Where will I be in 5 Years?

On the Subject of ME

MY BIO:

MY ACCOMPLISHMENTS:

BUSINESS PLANS:

Upcoming Events

MONTH:

DATE	EVENT	NOTES

Upcoming Events

MONTH:

DATE	EVENT	NOTES

Upcoming Events

MONTH:

DATE	EVENT	NOTES

Upcoming Events

MONTH:

DATE	EVENT	NOTES

Upcoming Events

MONTH:

DATE	EVENT	NOTES

Upcoming Events

MONTH:

DATE	EVENT	NOTES

Upcoming Events

MONTH:

DATE	EVENT	NOTES

Upcoming Events

MONTH:

DATE	EVENT	NOTES

Upcoming Events

MONTH:

DATE	EVENT	NOTES

Upcoming Events

MONTH:

DATE	EVENT	NOTES

Upcoming Events

MONTH:

DATE	EVENT	NOTES

Upcoming Events

MONTH:

DATE	EVENT	NOTES

3
2
10
9
HAIRDRESSER
17

MONTH:

Inside My Beautiful Head:

Workshops & Training:

New Products:

Positive Affirmations:

MONTH:

Inside My Beautiful Head:

WORKSHOPS & TRAINING:

NEW PRODUCTS:

POSITIVE AFFIRMATIONS:

MONTH:

Inside My Beautiful Head:

WORKSHOPS & TRAINING: ____________________

NEW PRODUCTS: ____________________

POSITIVE AFFIRMATIONS: ____________________

MONTH:

Inside My Beautiful Head:

WORKSHOPS & TRAINING:

NEW PRODUCTS:

POSITIVE AFFIRMATIONS:

MONTH:

Inside My Beautiful Head:

WORKSHOPS & TRAINING:

NEW PRODUCTS:

POSITIVE AFFIRMATIONS:

MONTH:

Inside My Beautiful Head:

WORKSHOPS & TRAINING:

NEW PRODUCTS:

POSITIVE AFFIRMATIONS:

Inside My Beautiful Head:

MONTH:

WORKSHOPS & TRAINING:

NEW PRODUCTS:

POSITIVE AFFIRMATIONS:

MONTH:

Inside My Beautiful Head:

WORKSHOPS & TRAINING:

NEW PRODUCTS:

POSITIVE AFFIRMATIONS:

MONTH:

Inside My Beautiful Head:

WORKSHOPS & TRAINING:

NEW PRODUCTS:

POSITIVE AFFIRMATIONS:

MONTH:

Inside My Beautiful Head:

WORKSHOPS & TRAINING:

NEW PRODUCTS:

POSITIVE AFFIRMATIONS:

MONTH:

Inside My Beautiful Head:

WORKSHOPS & TRAINING:

NEW PRODUCTS:

POSITIVE AFFIRMATIONS:

MONTH:

Inside My Beautiful Head:

WORKSHOPS & TRAINING:

NEW PRODUCTS:

POSITIVE AFFIRMATIONS:

"A woman who cuts
her hair
is about to change
her life."
- Coco Chanel

Important Phone Numbers and Email Addresses

Important Phone Numbers AND Email Addresses

Important Phone Numbers AND Email Addresses

Important Phone Numbers and Email Addresses

Important Phone Numbers AND Email Addresses

Important Phone Numbers and Email Addresses

Important Phone Numbers AND Email Addresses

Important Phone Numbers and Email Addresses

Important Phone Numbers AND Email Addresses

◈

◈

◈

◈

◈

◈

◈

◈

◈

Important Phone Numbers and Email Addresses

-
-
-
-
-
-
-
-
-

DAILY THINGS THAT MATTER

DATE: _______

MORNING	AFTERNOON	EVENING

DATE: _______

MORNING	AFTERNOON	EVENING

DATE: _______

MORNING	AFTERNOON	EVENING

DAILY THINGS THAT MATTER

DATE: _______

MORNING	AFTERNOON	EVENING
	-	-
	-	-
	-	-
	-	-
	-	-
	-	-
	-	-
	-	-

DATE: _______

MORNING	AFTERNOON	EVENING
	-	-
	-	-
	-	-
	-	-
	-	-
	-	-
	-	-
	-	-

DATE: _______

MORNING	AFTERNOON	EVENING
	-	-
	-	-
	-	-
	-	-
	-	-
	-	-
	-	-
	-	-

DAILY THINGS THAT MATTER

DATE: _______

MORNING	AFTERNOON	EVENING

DATE: _______

MORNING	AFTERNOON	EVENING

DATE: _______

MORNING	AFTERNOON	EVENING

DAILY THINGS THAT MATTER

DATE: _______

MORNING	AFTERNOON	EVENING

DATE: _______

MORNING	AFTERNOON	EVENING

DATE: _______

MORNING	AFTERNOON	EVENING

DAILY THINGS THAT MATTER

DATE: _______

MORNING	AFTERNOON	EVENING

DATE: _______

MORNING	AFTERNOON	EVENING

DATE: _______

MORNING	AFTERNOON	EVENING

DAILY THINGS THAT MATTER

DATE: _______

MORNING	AFTERNOON	EVENING

DATE: _______

MORNING	AFTERNOON	EVENING

DATE: _______

MORNING	AFTERNOON	EVENING

DAILY THINGS THAT MATTER

DATE: _______

MORNING	AFTERNOON	EVENING

DATE: _______

MORNING	AFTERNOON	EVENING

DATE: _______

MORNING	AFTERNOON	EVENING

DAILY THINGS THAT MATTER

DATE: _______

MORNING	AFTERNOON	EVENING

DATE: _______

MORNING	AFTERNOON	EVENING

DATE: _______

MORNING	AFTERNOON	EVENING

DAILY THINGS THAT MATTER

DATE: _______

MORNING	AFTERNOON	EVENING

DATE: _______

MORNING	AFTERNOON	EVENING

DATE: _______

MORNING	AFTERNOON	EVENING

DAILY THINGS THAT MATTER

DATE: _______

MORNING	AFTERNOON	EVENING
	-	-
	-	-
	-	-
	-	-
	-	-
	-	-
	-	-
	-	-

DATE: _______

MORNING	AFTERNOON	EVENING
	-	-
	-	-
	-	-
	-	-
	-	-
	-	-
	-	-
	-	-

DATE: _______

MORNING	AFTERNOON	EVENING
	-	-
	-	-
	-	-
	-	-
	-	-
	-	-
	-	-
	-	-

DAILY THINGS THAT MATTER

DATE: _______

MORNING	AFTERNOON	EVENING

DATE: _______

MORNING	AFTERNOON	EVENING

DATE: _______

MORNING	AFTERNOON	EVENING

DAILY THINGS THAT MATTER

DATE: _______

MORNING	AFTERNOON	EVENING

DATE: _______

MORNING	AFTERNOON	EVENING

DATE: _______

MORNING	AFTERNOON	EVENING

DAILY THINGS THAT MATTER

DATE: _______

MORNING	AFTERNOON	EVENING

DATE: _______

MORNING	AFTERNOON	EVENING

DATE: _______

MORNING	AFTERNOON	EVENING

DAILY THINGS THAT MATTER

DATE: _______

MORNING	AFTERNOON	EVENING

DATE: _______

MORNING	AFTERNOON	EVENING

DATE: _______

MORNING	AFTERNOON	EVENING

DAILY THINGS THAT MATTER

DATE: _______

MORNING	AFTERNOON	EVENING

DATE: _______

MORNING	AFTERNOON	EVENING

DATE: _______

MORNING	AFTERNOON	EVENING

DAILY THINGS THAT MATTER

DATE: _______

MORNING	AFTERNOON	EVENING

DATE: _______

MORNING	AFTERNOON	EVENING

DATE: _______

MORNING	AFTERNOON	EVENING

DAILY THINGS THAT MATTER

DATE: _______

MORNING **AFTERNOON** **EVENING**

DATE: _______

MORNING **AFTERNOON** **EVENING**

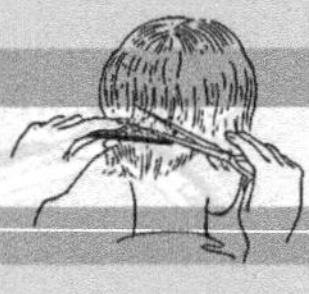

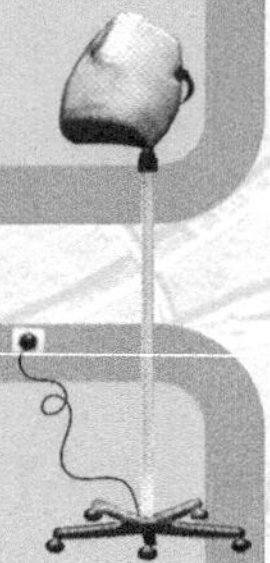

DATE: _______

MORNING **AFTERNOON** **EVENING**

DAILY THINGS THAT MATTER

DATE: _______

MORNING	AFTERNOON	EVENING
	-	-
	-	-
	-	-
	-	-
	-	-
	-	-
	-	-
	-	-

DATE: _______

MORNING	AFTERNOON	EVENING
	-	-
	-	-
	-	-
	-	-
	-	-
	-	-
	-	-
	-	-

DATE: _______

MORNING	AFTERNOON	EVENING
	-	-
	-	-
	-	-
	-	-
	-	-
	-	-
	-	-
	-	-

DAILY THINGS THAT MATTER

DATE: _______

MORNING	AFTERNOON	EVENING

DATE: _______

MORNING	AFTERNOON	EVENING

DATE: _______

MORNING	AFTERNOON	EVENING

DAILY THINGS THAT MATTER

DATE: _______

MORNING	AFTERNOON	EVENING

DATE: _______

MORNING	AFTERNOON	EVENING

DATE: _______

MORNING	AFTERNOON	EVENING

DAILY THINGS THAT MATTER

DATE: _______

MORNING	AFTERNOON	EVENING

DATE: _______

MORNING	AFTERNOON	EVENING

DATE: _______

MORNING	AFTERNOON	EVENING

DAILY THINGS THAT MATTER

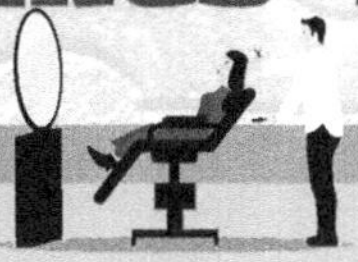

DATE: _______

MORNING	AFTERNOON	EVENING

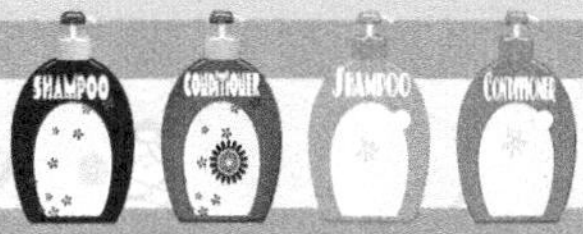

DATE: _______

MORNING	AFTERNOON	EVENING

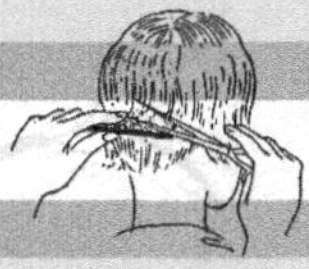

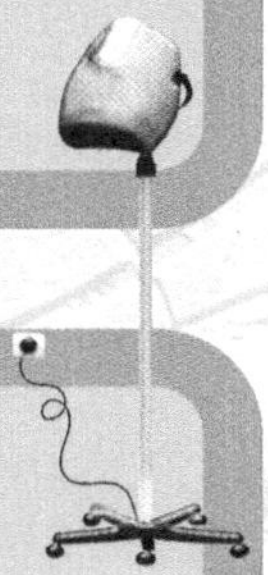

DATE: _______

MORNING	AFTERNOON	EVENING

DAILY THINGS THAT MATTER

DATE: _______

MORNING	AFTERNOON	EVENING

DATE: _______

MORNING	AFTERNOON	EVENING

DATE: _______

MORNING	AFTERNOON	EVENING

DAILY THINGS THAT MATTER

DATE: _______

MORNING	AFTERNOON	EVENING

DATE: _______

MORNING	AFTERNOON	EVENING

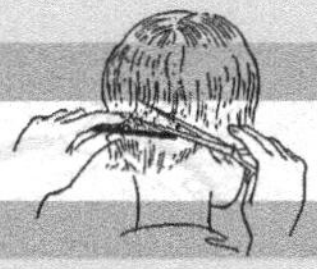
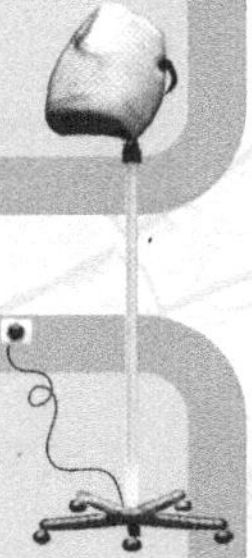

DATE: _______

MORNING	AFTERNOON	EVENING

DAILY THINGS THAT MATTER

DATE: _______

MORNING	AFTERNOON	EVENING

DATE: _______

MORNING	AFTERNOON	EVENING

DATE: _______

MORNING	AFTERNOON	EVENING

DAILY THINGS THAT MATTER

DATE: _______

MORNING	AFTERNOON	EVENING

DATE: _______

MORNING	AFTERNOON	EVENING

DATE: _______

MORNING	AFTERNOON	EVENING

DAILY THINGS THAT MATTER

DATE: _______

MORNING	AFTERNOON	EVENING
	-	-
	-	-
	-	-
	-	-
	-	-
	-	-
	-	-
	-	-

DATE: _______

MORNING	AFTERNOON	EVENING
	-	-
	-	-
	-	-
	-	-
	-	-
	-	-
	-	-
	-	-

DATE: _______

MORNING	AFTERNOON	EVENING
	-	-
	-	-
	-	-
	-	-
	-	-
	-	-
	-	-
	-	-

DAILY THINGS THAT MATTER

DATE: _______

MORNING	AFTERNOON	EVENING

DATE: _______

MORNING	AFTERNOON	EVENING

DATE: _______

MORNING	AFTERNOON	EVENING

DAILY THINGS THAT MATTER

DATE: _______

MORNING	AFTERNOON	EVENING

DATE: _______

MORNING	AFTERNOON	EVENING

DATE: _______

MORNING	AFTERNOON	EVENING

DAILY THINGS THAT MATTER

DATE: _______

MORNING | **AFTERNOON** | **EVENING**

DATE: _______

MORNING | **AFTERNOON** | **EVENING**

DATE: _______

MORNING | **AFTERNOON** | **EVENING**

DAILY THINGS THAT MATTER

DATE: _______

MORNING	AFTERNOON	EVENING

DATE: _______

MORNING	AFTERNOON	EVENING

DATE: _______

MORNING	AFTERNOON	EVENING

DAILY THINGS THAT MATTER

DATE: _______

MORNING	AFTERNOON	EVENING

DATE: _______

MORNING	AFTERNOON	EVENING

DATE: _______

MORNING	AFTERNOON	EVENING

DAILY THINGS THAT MATTER

DATE: _______

MORNING	AFTERNOON	EVENING

DATE: _______

MORNING	AFTERNOON	EVENING

DATE: _______

MORNING	AFTERNOON	EVENING

DAILY THINGS THAT MATTER

DATE: _______

MORNING	AFTERNOON	EVENING

DATE: _______

MORNING	AFTERNOON	EVENING

DATE: _______

MORNING	AFTERNOON	EVENING

DAILY THINGS THAT MATTER

DATE: _______

MORNING	AFTERNOON	EVENING

DATE: _______

MORNING	AFTERNOON	EVENING

DATE: _______

MORNING	AFTERNOON	EVENING

DAILY THINGS THAT MATTER

DATE: _______

MORNING	AFTERNOON	EVENING
	-	-
	-	-
	-	-
	-	-
	-	-
	-	-
	-	-
	-	-

DATE: _______

MORNING	AFTERNOON	EVENING
	-	-
	-	-
	-	-
	-	-
	-	-
	-	-
	-	-
	-	-

DATE: _______

MORNING	AFTERNOON	EVENING
	-	-
	-	-
	-	-
	-	-
	-	-
	-	-
	-	-
	-	-

DAILY THINGS THAT MATTER

DATE: _______

MORNING	AFTERNOON	EVENING

DATE: _______

MORNING	AFTERNOON	EVENING

DATE: _______

MORNING	AFTERNOON	EVENING

DAILY THINGS THAT MATTER

DATE: _______

MORNING	AFTERNOON	EVENING

DATE: _______

MORNING	AFTERNOON	EVENING

DATE: _______

MORNING	AFTERNOON	EVENING

DAILY THINGS THAT MATTER

DATE: _______

MORNING	AFTERNOON	EVENING

DATE: _______

MORNING	AFTERNOON	EVENING

DATE: _______

MORNING	AFTERNOON	EVENING

DAILY THINGS THAT MATTER

DATE: _______

MORNING	AFTERNOON	EVENING

DATE: _______

MORNING	AFTERNOON	EVENING

DATE: _______

MORNING	AFTERNOON	EVENING

DAILY THINGS THAT MATTER

DATE: _______

MORNING	AFTERNOON	EVENING

DATE: _______

MORNING	AFTERNOON	EVENING

DATE: _______

MORNING	AFTERNOON	EVENING

DAILY THINGS THAT MATTER

DATE: _______

MORNING	AFTERNOON	EVENING

DATE: _______

MORNING	AFTERNOON	EVENING

DATE: _______

MORNING	AFTERNOON	EVENING

DAILY THINGS THAT MATTER

DATE: _______

MORNING	AFTERNOON	EVENING

DATE: _______

MORNING	AFTERNOON	EVENING

DATE: _______

MORNING	AFTERNOON	EVENING

DAILY THINGS THAT MATTER

DATE: _______

MORNING	AFTERNOON	EVENING

DATE: _______

MORNING	AFTERNOON	EVENING

DATE: _______

MORNING	AFTERNOON	EVENING

DAILY THINGS THAT MATTER

DATE: _______

MORNING	AFTERNOON	EVENING

DATE: _______

MORNING	AFTERNOON	EVENING

DATE: _______

MORNING	AFTERNOON	EVENING

DAILY THINGS THAT MATTER

DATE: _______

MORNING	AFTERNOON	EVENING

DATE: _______

MORNING	AFTERNOON	EVENING

DATE: _______

MORNING	AFTERNOON	EVENING

DAILY THINGS THAT MATTER

DATE: _______

MORNING	AFTERNOON	EVENING

DATE: _______

MORNING	AFTERNOON	EVENING

DATE: _______

MORNING	AFTERNOON	EVENING

DAILY THINGS THAT MATTER

DATE: _______

MORNING	AFTERNOON	EVENING
	-	-
	-	-
	-	-
	-	-
	-	-
	-	-
	-	-
	-	-

DATE: _______

MORNING	AFTERNOON	EVENING
	-	-
	-	-
	-	-
	-	-
	-	-
	-	-
	-	-
	-	-

DATE: _______

MORNING	AFTERNOON	EVENING
	-	-
	-	-
	-	-
	-	-
	-	-
	-	-
	-	-
	-	-

DAILY THINGS THAT MATTER

DATE: _______

MORNING	AFTERNOON	EVENING

DATE: _______

MORNING	AFTERNOON	EVENING

DATE: _______

MORNING	AFTERNOON	EVENING

DAILY THINGS THAT MATTER

DATE: _______

MORNING	AFTERNOON	EVENING

DATE: _______

MORNING	AFTERNOON	EVENING

DATE: _______

MORNING	AFTERNOON	EVENING

DAILY THINGS THAT MATTER

DATE: _______

MORNING	AFTERNOON	EVENING

DATE: _______

MORNING	AFTERNOON	EVENING

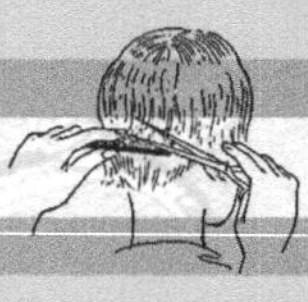

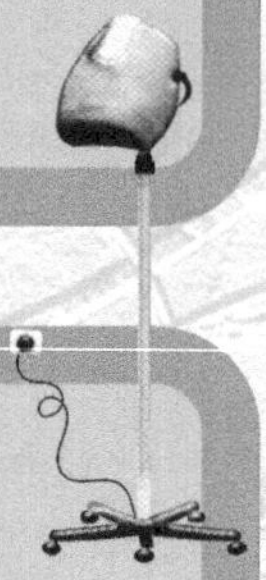

DATE: _______

MORNING	AFTERNOON	EVENING

DAILY THINGS THAT MATTER

DATE: _______

MORNING	AFTERNOON	EVENING

DATE: _______

MORNING	AFTERNOON	EVENING

DATE: _______

MORNING	AFTERNOON	EVENING

DAILY THINGS THAT MATTER

DATE: _______

MORNING | AFTERNOON | EVENING

DATE: _______

MORNING | AFTERNOON | EVENING

DATE: _______

MORNING | AFTERNOON | EVENING

DAILY THINGS THAT MATTER

DATE: _______

MORNING	AFTERNOON	EVENING

DATE: _______

MORNING	AFTERNOON	EVENING

DATE: _______

MORNING	AFTERNOON	EVENING

DAILY THINGS THAT MATTER

DATE: _______

MORNING	AFTERNOON	EVENING

DATE: _______

MORNING	AFTERNOON	EVENING

DATE: _______

MORNING	AFTERNOON	EVENING

DAILY THINGS THAT MATTER

DATE: _______

MORNING	AFTERNOON	EVENING

DATE: _______

MORNING	AFTERNOON	EVENING

DATE: _______

MORNING	AFTERNOON	EVENING

DAILY THINGS THAT MATTER

DATE: _______

MORNING	AFTERNOON	EVENING

DATE: _______

MORNING	AFTERNOON	EVENING

DATE: _______

MORNING	AFTERNOON	EVENING

DAILY THINGS THAT MATTER

DATE: _______

MORNING	AFTERNOON	EVENING

DATE: _______

MORNING	AFTERNOON	EVENING

DATE: _______

MORNING	AFTERNOON	EVENING

DAILY THINGS THAT MATTER

DATE: _______

MORNING	AFTERNOON	EVENING

DATE: _______

MORNING	AFTERNOON	EVENING

DATE: _______

MORNING	AFTERNOON	EVENING

DAILY THINGS THAT MATTER

DATE: _______

MORNING	AFTERNOON	EVENING

DATE: _______

MORNING	AFTERNOON	EVENING

DATE: _______

MORNING	AFTERNOON	EVENING

DAILY THINGS THAT MATTER

DATE: _______

MORNING	AFTERNOON	EVENING

DATE: _______

MORNING	AFTERNOON	EVENING

DATE: _______

MORNING	AFTERNOON	EVENING

DAILY THINGS THAT MATTER

DATE: _______

MORNING	AFTERNOON	EVENING

DATE: _______

MORNING	AFTERNOON	EVENING

DATE: _______

MORNING	AFTERNOON	EVENING

DAILY THINGS THAT MATTER

DATE: _______

MORNING	AFTERNOON	EVENING

DATE: _______

MORNING	AFTERNOON	EVENING

DATE: _______

MORNING	AFTERNOON	EVENING

DAILY THINGS THAT MATTER

DATE: _______

MORNING	AFTERNOON	EVENING

DATE: _______

MORNING	AFTERNOON	EVENING

DATE: _______

MORNING	AFTERNOON	EVENING

DAILY THINGS THAT MATTER

DATE: _______

MORNING	AFTERNOON	EVENING
	-	-
	-	-
	-	-
	-	-
	-	-
	-	-
	-	-
	-	-

DATE: _______

MORNING	AFTERNOON	EVENING
	-	-
	-	-
	-	-
	-	-
	-	-
	-	-
	-	-
	-	-

DATE: _______

MORNING	AFTERNOON	EVENING
	-	-
	-	-
	-	-
	-	-
	-	-
	-	-
	-	-
	-	-

DAILY THINGS THAT MATTER

DATE: _______

MORNING	AFTERNOON	EVENING

DATE: _______

MORNING	AFTERNOON	EVENING

DATE: _______

MORNING	AFTERNOON	EVENING

DAILY THINGS THAT MATTER

DATE: _______

MORNING	AFTERNOON	EVENING

DATE: _______

MORNING	AFTERNOON	EVENING

DATE: _______

MORNING	AFTERNOON	EVENING

DAILY THINGS THAT MATTER

DATE: _______

MORNING	AFTERNOON	EVENING

DATE: _______

MORNING	AFTERNOON	EVENING

DATE: _______

MORNING	AFTERNOON	EVENING

DAILY THINGS THAT MATTER

DATE: _______

MORNING	AFTERNOON	EVENING

DATE: _______

MORNING	AFTERNOON	EVENING

DATE: _______

MORNING	AFTERNOON	EVENING

DAILY THINGS THAT MATTER

DATE: _______

MORNING	AFTERNOON	EVENING

DATE: _______

MORNING	AFTERNOON	EVENING

DATE: _______

MORNING	AFTERNOON	EVENING

DAILY THINGS THAT MATTER

DATE: _______

MORNING	AFTERNOON	EVENING

DATE: _______

MORNING	AFTERNOON	EVENING

DATE: _______

MORNING	AFTERNOON	EVENING

DAILY THINGS THAT MATTER

DATE: _______

MORNING	AFTERNOON	EVENING

DATE: _______

MORNING	AFTERNOON	EVENING

DATE: _______

MORNING	AFTERNOON	EVENING

DAILY THINGS THAT MATTER

DATE: _______

MORNING	AFTERNOON	EVENING
	-	-
	-	-
	-	-
	-	-
	-	-
	-	-
	-	-
	-	-

DATE: _______

MORNING	AFTERNOON	EVENING
	-	-
	-	-
	-	-
	-	-
	-	-
	-	-
	-	-
	-	-

DATE: _______

MORNING	AFTERNOON	EVENING
	-	-
	-	-
	-	-
	-	-
	-	-
	-	-
	-	-
	-	-

DAILY THINGS THAT MATTER

DATE: _______

MORNING	AFTERNOON	EVENING

DATE: _______

MORNING	AFTERNOON	EVENING

DATE: _______

MORNING	AFTERNOON	EVENING

DAILY THINGS THAT MATTER

DATE: _______

MORNING	AFTERNOON	EVENING

DATE: _______

MORNING	AFTERNOON	EVENING

DATE: _______

MORNING	AFTERNOON	EVENING

DAILY THINGS THAT MATTER

DATE: _______

MORNING	AFTERNOON	EVENING

DATE: _______

MORNING	AFTERNOON	EVENING

DATE: _______

MORNING	AFTERNOON	EVENING

DAILY THINGS THAT MATTER

DATE: _______

MORNING	AFTERNOON	EVENING
	-	-
	-	-
	-	-
	-	-
	-	-
	-	-
	-	-
	-	-

DATE: _______

MORNING	AFTERNOON	EVENING
	-	-
	-	-
	-	-
	-	-
	-	-
	-	-
	-	-
	-	-

DATE: _______

MORNING	AFTERNOON	EVENING
	-	-
	-	-
	-	-
	-	-
	-	-
	-	-
	-	-
	-	-

DAILY THINGS THAT MATTER

DATE: _______

MORNING	AFTERNOON	EVENING

DATE: _______

MORNING	AFTERNOON	EVENING

DATE: _______

MORNING	AFTERNOON	EVENING

DAILY THINGS THAT MATTER

DATE: _______

MORNING	AFTERNOON	EVENING

DATE: _______

MORNING	AFTERNOON	EVENING

DATE: _______

MORNING	AFTERNOON	EVENING

DAILY THINGS THAT MATTER

DATE: _______

MORNING	AFTERNOON	EVENING

DATE: _______

MORNING	AFTERNOON	EVENING

DATE: _______

MORNING	AFTERNOON	EVENING

DAILY THINGS THAT MATTER

DATE: _______

MORNING	AFTERNOON	EVENING
	-	-
	-	-
	-	-
	-	-
	-	-
	-	-
	-	-
	-	-

DATE: _______

MORNING	AFTERNOON	EVENING
	-	-
	-	-
	-	-
	-	-
	-	-
	-	-
	-	-
	-	-

DATE: _______

MORNING	AFTERNOON	EVENING
	-	-
	-	-
	-	-
	-	-
	-	-
	-	-
	-	-
	-	-

DAILY THINGS THAT MATTER

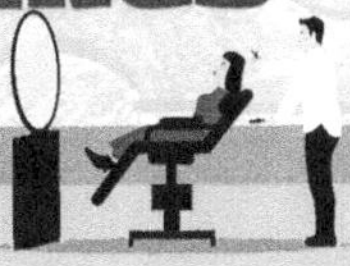

DATE: _______

MORNING	AFTERNOON	EVENING

DATE: _______

MORNING	AFTERNOON	EVENING

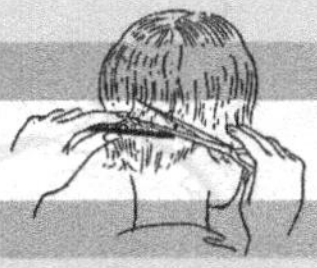

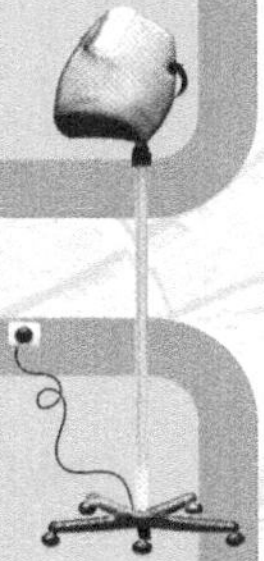

DATE: _______

MORNING	AFTERNOON	EVENING

DAILY THINGS THAT MATTER

DATE: _______

MORNING	AFTERNOON	EVENING

DATE: _______

MORNING	AFTERNOON	EVENING

DATE: _______

MORNING	AFTERNOON	EVENING

DAILY THINGS THAT MATTER

DATE: _______

MORNING	AFTERNOON	EVENING

DATE: _______

MORNING	AFTERNOON	EVENING

DATE: _______

MORNING	AFTERNOON	EVENING

DAILY THINGS THAT MATTER

DATE: _______

MORNING | **AFTERNOON** | **EVENING**

DATE: _______

MORNING | **AFTERNOON** | **EVENING**

DATE: _______

MORNING | **AFTERNOON** | **EVENING**

DAILY THINGS THAT MATTER

DATE: _______

MORNING	AFTERNOON	EVENING

DATE: _______

MORNING	AFTERNOON	EVENING

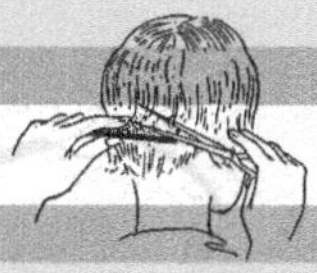

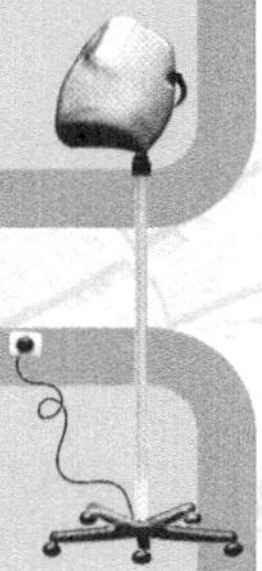

DATE: _______

MORNING	AFTERNOON	EVENING

DAILY THINGS THAT MATTER

DATE: _______

MORNING	AFTERNOON	EVENING

DATE: _______

MORNING	AFTERNOON	EVENING

DATE: _______

MORNING	AFTERNOON	EVENING

DAILY THINGS THAT MATTER

DATE: _______

MORNING	AFTERNOON	EVENING

DATE: _______

MORNING	AFTERNOON	EVENING

DATE: _______

MORNING	AFTERNOON	EVENING

DAILY THINGS THAT MATTER

DATE: _______

MORNING	AFTERNOON	EVENING

DATE: _______

MORNING	AFTERNOON	EVENING

DATE: _______

MORNING	AFTERNOON	EVENING

DAILY THINGS THAT MATTER

DATE: _______

MORNING	AFTERNOON	EVENING

DATE: _______

MORNING	AFTERNOON	EVENING

DATE: _______

MORNING	AFTERNOON	EVENING

DAILY THINGS THAT MATTER

DATE: _______

MORNING	AFTERNOON	EVENING
	-	-
	-	-
	-	-
	-	-
	-	-
	-	-
	-	-
	-	-

DATE: _______

MORNING	AFTERNOON	EVENING
	-	-
	-	-
	-	-
	-	-
	-	-
	-	-
	-	-
	-	-

DATE: _______

MORNING	AFTERNOON	EVENING
	-	-
	-	-
	-	-
	-	-
	-	-
	-	-
	-	-
	-	-

DAILY THINGS THAT MATTER

DATE: _______

MORNING	AFTERNOON	EVENING

DATE: _______

MORNING	AFTERNOON	EVENING

DATE: _______

MORNING	AFTERNOON	EVENING

DAILY THINGS THAT MATTER

DATE: _______

MORNING	AFTERNOON	EVENING

DATE: _______

MORNING	AFTERNOON	EVENING

DATE: _______

MORNING	AFTERNOON	EVENING

DAILY THINGS THAT MATTER

DATE: _______

MORNING	AFTERNOON	EVENING

DATE: _______

MORNING	AFTERNOON	EVENING

DATE: _______

MORNING	AFTERNOON	EVENING

DAILY THINGS THAT MATTER

DATE: _______

MORNING	AFTERNOON	EVENING

DATE: _______

MORNING	AFTERNOON	EVENING

DATE: _______

MORNING	AFTERNOON	EVENING

DAILY THINGS THAT MATTER

DATE: _______

MORNING	AFTERNOON	EVENING

DATE: _______

MORNING	AFTERNOON	EVENING

DATE: _______

MORNING	AFTERNOON	EVENING

DAILY THINGS THAT MATTER

DATE: _______

MORNING	AFTERNOON	EVENING

DATE: _______

MORNING	AFTERNOON	EVENING

DATE: _______

MORNING	AFTERNOON	EVENING

DAILY THINGS THAT MATTER

DATE: _______

MORNING	AFTERNOON	EVENING
	-	-
	-	-
	-	-
	-	-
	-	-
	-	-
	-	-
	-	-

DATE: _______

MORNING	AFTERNOON	EVENING
	-	-
	-	-
	-	-
	-	-
	-	-
	-	-
	-	-
	-	-

DATE: _______

MORNING	AFTERNOON	EVENING
	-	-
	-	-
	-	-
	-	-
	-	-
	-	-
	-	-
	-	-

DAILY THINGS THAT MATTER

DATE: _______

MORNING	AFTERNOON	EVENING

DATE: _______

MORNING	AFTERNOON	EVENING

DATE: _______

MORNING	AFTERNOON	EVENING

DAILY THINGS THAT MATTER

DATE: _______

MORNING	AFTERNOON	EVENING

DATE: _______

MORNING	AFTERNOON	EVENING

DATE: _______

MORNING	AFTERNOON	EVENING

DAILY THINGS THAT MATTER

DATE: _______

MORNING	AFTERNOON	EVENING

DATE: _______

MORNING	AFTERNOON	EVENING

DATE: _______

MORNING	AFTERNOON	EVENING

DAILY THINGS THAT MATTER

DATE: _______

MORNING	AFTERNOON	EVENING

DATE: _______

MORNING	AFTERNOON	EVENING

DATE: _______

MORNING	AFTERNOON	EVENING

DAILY THINGS THAT MATTER

DATE: _______

MORNING	AFTERNOON	EVENING

DATE: _______

MORNING	AFTERNOON	EVENING

DATE: _______

MORNING	AFTERNOON	EVENING

DAILY THINGS THAT MATTER

DATE: _______

MORNING	AFTERNOON	EVENING

DATE: _______

MORNING	AFTERNOON	EVENING

DATE: _______

MORNING	AFTERNOON	EVENING

DAILY THINGS THAT MATTER

DATE: _______

MORNING	AFTERNOON	EVENING

DATE: _______

MORNING	AFTERNOON	EVENING

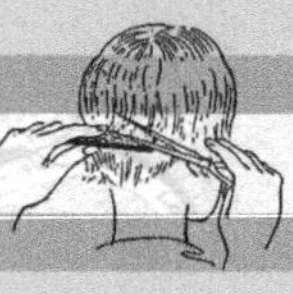

DATE: _______

MORNING	AFTERNOON	EVENING

DAILY THINGS THAT MATTER

DATE: _______

MORNING	AFTERNOON	EVENING

DATE: _______

MORNING	AFTERNOON	EVENING

DATE: _______

MORNING	AFTERNOON	EVENING

DAILY THINGS THAT MATTER

DATE: _______

MORNING	AFTERNOON	EVENING

DATE: _______

MORNING	AFTERNOON	EVENING

DATE: _______

MORNING	AFTERNOON	EVENING

DAILY THINGS THAT MATTER

DATE: _______

MORNING	AFTERNOON	EVENING

DATE: _______

MORNING	AFTERNOON	EVENING

DATE: _______

MORNING	AFTERNOON	EVENING

DAILY THINGS THAT MATTER

DATE: _______

MORNING	AFTERNOON	EVENING

DATE: _______

MORNING	AFTERNOON	EVENING

DATE: _______

MORNING	AFTERNOON	EVENING

DAILY THINGS THAT MATTER

DATE: _______

MORNING	AFTERNOON	EVENING

DATE: _______

MORNING	AFTERNOON	EVENING

DATE: _______

MORNING	AFTERNOON	EVENING

DAILY THINGS THAT MATTER

DATE: _______

MORNING | AFTERNOON | EVENING

DATE: _______

MORNING | AFTERNOON | EVENING

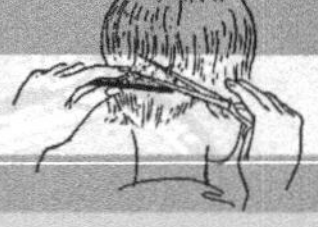

DATE: _______

MORNING | AFTERNOON | EVENING

DAILY THINGS THAT MATTER

DATE: _______

MORNING	AFTERNOON	EVENING

DATE: _______

MORNING	AFTERNOON	EVENING

DATE: _______

MORNING	AFTERNOON	EVENING

DAILY THINGS THAT MATTER

DATE: _______

MORNING **AFTERNOON** **EVENING**

DATE: _______

MORNING **AFTERNOON** **EVENING**

DATE: _______

MORNING **AFTERNOON** **EVENING**

DAILY THINGS THAT MATTER

DATE: _______

MORNING	AFTERNOON	EVENING
	-	-
	-	-
	-	-
	-	-
	-	-
	-	-
	-	-
	-	-

DATE: _______

MORNING	AFTERNOON	EVENING
	-	-
	-	-
	-	-
	-	-
	-	-
	-	-
	-	-
	-	-

DATE: _______

MORNING	AFTERNOON	EVENING
	-	-
	-	-
	-	-
	-	-
	-	-
	-	-
	-	-
	-	-

DAILY THINGS THAT MATTER

DATE: _______

MORNING	AFTERNOON	EVENING

DATE: _______

MORNING	AFTERNOON	EVENING

DATE: _______

MORNING	AFTERNOON	EVENING

DAILY THINGS THAT MATTER

DATE: _______

MORNING	AFTERNOON	EVENING

DATE: _______

MORNING	AFTERNOON	EVENING

DATE: _______

MORNING	AFTERNOON	EVENING

DAILY THINGS THAT MATTER

DATE: _______

MORNING	AFTERNOON	EVENING

DATE: _______

MORNING	AFTERNOON	EVENING

DATE: _______

MORNING	AFTERNOON	EVENING

DAILY THINGS THAT MATTER

DATE: _______

MORNING	AFTERNOON	EVENING

DATE: _______

MORNING	AFTERNOON	EVENING

DATE: _______

MORNING	AFTERNOON	EVENING

DAILY THINGS THAT MATTER

DATE: _______

MORNING	AFTERNOON	EVENING

DATE: _______

MORNING	AFTERNOON	EVENING

DATE: _______

MORNING	AFTERNOON	EVENING

DAILY THINGS THAT MATTER

DATE: _______

MORNING	AFTERNOON	EVENING

DATE: _______

MORNING	AFTERNOON	EVENING

DATE: _______

MORNING	AFTERNOON	EVENING

DAILY THINGS THAT MATTER

DATE: _______

MORNING	AFTERNOON	EVENING

DATE: _______

MORNING	AFTERNOON	EVENING

DATE: _______

MORNING	AFTERNOON	EVENING

DAILY THINGS THAT MATTER

DATE: _______

MORNING	AFTERNOON	EVENING

DATE: _______

MORNING	AFTERNOON	EVENING

DATE: _______

MORNING	AFTERNOON	EVENING

P.S I Love You

Made in the USA
Middletown, DE
05 November 2026

36544878R10117